Justin
Bieber

BIEBER FEVER!

Contents

Published by World Publications Group, Inc.
140 Laurel Street
East Bridgewater, MA 02333
www.wrldpub.com

© Instinctive Product Development 2013

Packaged by Instinctive Product Development for World Publications Group, Inc.

Printed in China

ISBN: 978-1-4643-0180-3

Designed by: BrainWave

Creative Director: Kevin Gardner

Written by: Jessica Toyne

Images courtesy of PA Photos

Introduction

In 2007, a 12-year-old boy entered the Stratford Idol singing competition, a youth center contest inspired by *American Idol*. Performing a cover of Ne-Yo's *So Sick*, the young Justin Bieber impressed the judges and won second place, despite having no formal musical or vocal coaching.

Justin and his mother, Pattie Mallette, had wanted to share the young singer's musical talents with friends and family and began uploading home videos on to *YouTube*. Little did they know that this simple act would be the start of a global phenomenon. With a rich talent at such a tender age, more and more people began subscribing to Bieber's *YouTube* channel and asked for more.

Fast-forward a year and Scooter Braun, a former marketing executive, stumbles across the *YouTube* videos of a bright, good-looking teen with a pure and clear voice singing his heart out.

Realizing that there was untapped talent right in front of him, he made contact with the Bieber family and a meeting was arranged. Scooter Braun organized to fly Justin out to Atlanta to record a demo and meet with R&B singer-songwriter Usher. Justin then went on to sign to Raymond Braun Media Group (RBMG) before signing to Island Records in the fall of 2008.

After bursting onto the music scene in the summer of 2009, Justin Bieber quickly became a household name who was adored by millions and was especially popular with his teen following: The "Beliebers."

His fame reached dizzying

■ **BELOW: Justin with his manager Scooter Braun.**

heights within just the first year of his career; his debut album was certified Platinum in the United States and Double Platinum in Canada and the United Kingdom. Justin also performed for US President Barack Obama and First Lady Michelle Obama at the White House for *Christmas in Washington*, which was broadcast on December 20, 2009 by TNT.

Justin Bieber owes much of his success to social media and it's not surprising to see that he utilizes it to the max. With more than 28 million followers on Twitter, he is the second most popular celebrity through this media and is listed in the top-10

■ ABOVE: Jennifer Nettles (left), Kristian Bush, Mary
J. Blige, President Barack Obama and First Lady
Michelle Obama, George Lopez, and Justin sing
during Christmas in Washington.

■ **ABOVE: Justin in his guest starring role on *CSI*.**

musicians' pages on Facebook. His original *YouTube* channel has over 1.6 million subscribers with more than 440 million videos viewed, and his official *YouTube* channel *JustinBieberVEVO* has over 1.9 million subscribers with more than 2.9 billion video views. Not bad for just three years in the spotlight!

Early videos of Justin can still be seen on *YouTube* today under the original user name "Kidrauhl," showing footage of a small boy busking on the steps of the Avon Theater in his hometown of Stratford, as well as dozens of home videos of Justin playing piano, guitar, and singing the songs by his favorite artists.

Bieber's success has grown year on year with millions of loyal fans or "Beliebers" remaining loyal to him. Over the course of the past three years his music has matured along with the young singer and his fan base.

Justin Bieber has sold over 15 million albums worldwide, completed two world tours, released his feature length movie (*Justin Bieber: Never Say Never*), and has been a guest star on *CSI: Crime Scene Investigation*. He has become one of the most talked about teens of the 21st century. Alongside this, Bieber has donated millions of dollars to various charities around the world and has been an active fundraiser, using his celebrity status to help change the world for the better. Justin Bieber truly has touched the lives of millions.

This fact-packed book offers everything you need to know about one of the world's most idolized teens, as well as filling you in with plenty of gossip, trivia, and photos of a global superstar that has infected the world with Bieber Fever.

Profile

Name: Justin Drew Bieber

Date of Birth: March 1, 1994

Place of Birth: London, Ontario, Canada

Star Sign: Pisces

Eye Color: Brown

Religion: Christian

Nationality: Canadian

Parents: Pattie Mallette and Jeremy Jack Bieber

Siblings: Half-sister Jazmyn Bieber and half-brother Jaxon Bieber

Nicknames: J-Beebs, Bieber, Biebs, JB, J-Biebs

Sports and Hobbies: Ice Hockey, Skateboarding, Chess

Musical Instruments: Drums, Guitar, Trumpet, Piano

Favorite Color: Purple

Favorite Food: Spaghetti and meatballs

Favorite Animal: Giraffe

Biography

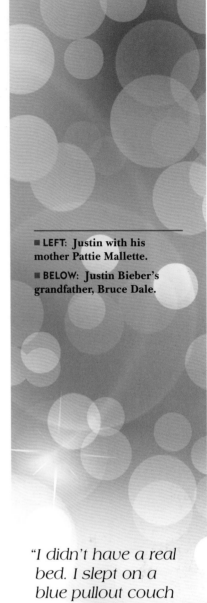

■ **LEFT: Justin with his mother Pattie Mallette.**

■ **BELOW: Justin Bieber's grandfather, Bruce Dale.**

Early Life

Justin Drew Bieber was born on March 1, 1994 in London, Ontario, Canada, at St Joseph's Hospital. Pattie Mallette, as a young single mother who at just 17 had become pregnant, raised Justin in Stratford, Ontario. Justin's parents had never been married and separated while he was only a baby. Justin's father Jeremy Bieber went on to marry another woman and had two children: Jaxon and Jazmyn.

Justin had a very modest upbringing, with his mother working a series of low-paying office jobs and living in low-income housing. When times got really tough, Justin and his mother moved in with her parents Bruce and Diane who offered help and support to the young family.

Justin was an active youth who enjoyed spending his time playing soccer and chess. He was bullied as a youngster because he was short so his grandfather Bruce inspired and encouraged him to play ice hockey; although small, Justin was nimble and the experience of playing ice hockey gave him a fighting spirit.

His love for music began at an early age when, at just four years old, he was given a drum kit. Even when he was a toddler, Justin's mom recalls how he would "tap and bang" anything to make simple rhythms and she encouraged Justin to play. With tips from the local church, and youthful determination, he enthusiastically taught himself how to master the drums. His dedication continued when, at eight years old, he started to play guitar. His creative ambition drove him to pick up an instrument that his mother had at home. Being left handed, this presented a new challenge when he realized he would need a left-handed guitar but, as soon as this was resolved, Justin was well on his way to accompanying himself.

"I didn't have a real bed. I slept on a blue pullout couch in my room."

From Competition to Career

At 12 years old, Justin entered the Stratford Idol singing contest held at the local Kiwanis Community Center. Performing a cover of Ne-Yo's *So Sick*, Justin took second place, even though he was a novice performer up against singers who had benefited from vocal training. Music was a massive part of his life right from this early age and, long before the days of a record deal, he would take his acoustic guitar out and busk his favorite songs in Stratford.

As he grew up, Justin's love for music also grew. When watching Michael Jackson and Justin Timberlake videos he realized that this was where he desired to be – on stage, in the spotlight, performing to an audience of thousands. His experience at the Stratford Idol contest had given him his first adrenaline-fueled taste of stage performance and he wanted more.

Being a teen of the digital age, Justin had a valuable tool right at his fingertips. With the unique power of *YouTube* he was able to upload videos of himself singing his favorite songs, while beginning to share his musical talent. Little did he know that this was the start of his whirlwind journey to stardom.

Meanwhile, miles away in Atlanta, Scott "Scooter" Braun, a former marketing executive of So So Def Records, was scouting the internet for another singer. After accidently clicking on one of Justin's *YouTube* videos, he quickly realized that here in front of him was young, untapped talent. After tracking him down through the *MySpace* social networking site, Scooter Braun

■ **ABOVE: Justin shares a joke with Scooter Braun.**

■ **OPPOSITE: Justin pictured with Usher.**

■ **BELOW: Justin poses with members of the Jackson family, after the hand and footprint ceremony honoring Michael Jackson, in front of Grauman's Chinese Theatre in Los Angeles.**

contacted the Bieber family and, after much persuasion, arranged to fly Justin out to Atlanta to meet Scooter and international rap star and singer-songwriter Usher. Not only was the trip Bieber's first visit to the US, but it was also his first time on an airplane.

Justin Bieber spoke about this first trip to Atlanta: *"Right when we flew into Atlanta, Scooter drove us to the studio and Usher was there in the parking lot. That was my first time ever being out of Canada so I went up to him and was like, 'Hey Usher, I love your songs, do you want me to sing you one?' He was like, 'No little buddy, just come inside, it's cold out.'"* A week later, and Justin returned to Atlanta to perform for Usher. *"I sang for him and his people and he really wanted to sign me then and there but I still had a meeting with Justin Timberlake who also wanted to sign me. It turned out Usher's deal was way better."*

Justin Bieber signed to Raymond Braun Media Group, a joint venture between Usher and Scooter Braun, and then, later in October 2008, he officially signed to Island Records. Being a signed artist soon became a full-time job for the singer, but that didn't mean he could give up his studies! Like many other teen and child stars, Justin started home schooling and even had tutors take to the road with him to ensure that he got an education. He also continued with his sporting ambitions and played hockey for the Atlanta Knights.

The early days of Bieber's career were spent working with songwriters and producers in order to get the young singer comfortable in the studio environment. Producing a first-rate pop star required an extensive team of musicians, producers, and songwriters, as well as personnel to take care of legal affairs, marketing, and styling.

His first single *One Time* was released in July 2009 while the remainder of the EP was being recorded.

■ **ABOVE: Justin Timberlake, who wanted to sign Bieber.**

14

All Around The World

Justin Bieber has become a global sensation, with his popularity growing across America, Europe, Australia, and Asia. We take a look at the musical journey the singer has embarked upon, including album and single releases, tours, awards, and his feature-length biopic *Never Say Never*.

Discography

November 2009: *My World* (EP)
March 2010: *My World 2.0*
November 2010: *My Worlds: The Collection*
November 2010: *My Worlds Acoustic*
February 2011: *Never Say Never: The Remixes*
November 2011: *Under The Mistletoe*
June 2012: *Believe*

Singles:

One Time
One Less Lonely Girl
Baby
Eenie Meenie
Somebody To Love
U Smile
Pray
Never Say Never
Mistletoe
Boyfriend
As Long As You Love Me
Beauty And A Beat

My World (Extended Play)

Released: November 17, 2009 No. 1 in Canada and reached top-10 album charts in France, Germany, Ireland, United States, United Kingdom, New Zealand
Canada and United Kingdom: Certified Double Platinum
United States: Certified Platinum

My World was released on November 17, 2009 and was the first of a two-part debut release. The seven-track extended play (EP) was released via Island Records as a prelude to the album *My World 2.0*.

The album was positively received by the public and peaked at No. 5 on the *Billboard 200*, selling 137,000 copies in its first week. *My World* went on to become certified Platinum in the US after selling over one million copies and went Double Platinum in the UK.

It debuted at No. 1 on the Canadian Albums Chart and was certified Platinum in less than a month after its release.

Working with a variety of producers gave the album an R&B-influenced sound. Bieber worked closely with his mentor Usher, who is well known for his international success with

RIAA diamond certified album *Confessions* in 2004.

The production team also included The-Dream and Tricky Stewart who are noted for co-writing and producing chart-topping singles such as Rihanna's *Umbrella* and Beyoncé's *Single Ladies (Put A Ring On It)*. The album possesses a balance of upbeat synth-driven mainstream R&B-infused pop, with tracks such as *One Time, Bigger,* and *Favorite Girl*, and groovy pop ballads with subtle R&B undertones with tracks *Down To Earth* and *First Dance*.

The album is largely based on coming of age and teen romance. When discussing the track *Down To Earth* in an interview with *Billboard*, Bieber said: *"It's a ballad about the feelings I had when my parents split up and how I helped my family get through it. I think a lot of kids have had their parents split up, and they should know that it wasn't because of something they did. I hope people can relate to it."*

Prior to the album's release, JB became the first solo artist in *Billboard* history to have at least four singles enter the top 40 of the Hot 100 before his debut album's release. The lead single *One Time* was released on July 7, 2009 and reached the top 20 in Canada, the US, Germany, the UK, France, and New Zealand. The music video for *One Time* was posted on Bieber's *YouTube* channel a month prior to release and within six months had achieved more than 100 million views.

Subsequent singles from the *My World* EP were released exclusively on iTunes. *One Less Lonely Girl* was released on October 6, 2009, which was closely followed by two further promotional singles *Love Me*, released on October 26,

2009 and *Favorite Girl*, released on November 3, 2009. Promotion for the album included a short tour sponsored by clothing retailer Urban Behavior.

Track Listing:

One Time
Favorite Girl
Down to Earth
Bigger
One Less Lonely Girl
First Dance
Love Me

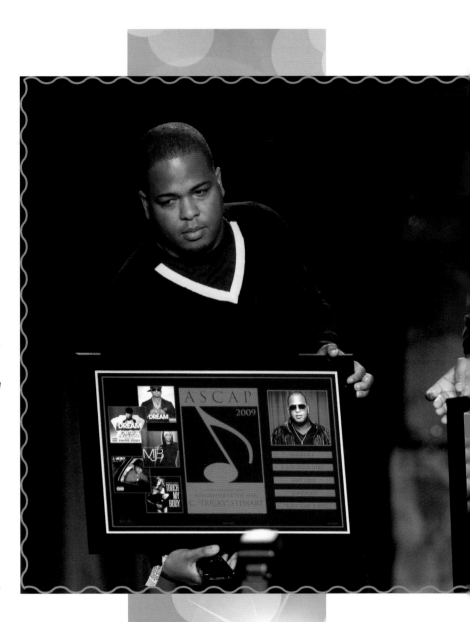

■ ABOVE: Tricky Stewart, left, and The-Dream accept the Songwriters of the Year award in 2009.

18

My World 2.0

Released: March 23, 2010
No. 1 in United States, Canada,
New Zealand, Australia
Canada: Certified Double
Platinum
United States: Certified Triple
Platinum
Australia: Certified Triple Platinum
Austria: Certified Gold
New Zealand: Certified Platinum

Track Listing:
Baby (ft. Ludacris)
Somebody To Love
Stuck In The Moment
U Smile
Runaway Love
Never Let You Go
Overboard
Eenie Meenie
Up
That Should Be Me

My World 2.0 released on March 23, 2010, is the follow-up album of the two-part debut release. Following in the footsteps of the EP *My World*, *My World 2.0* features a pop-inspired R&B sound with the addition of a hip-hop influence, which has been described as creating an edgier and more mature sound.

After the successful collaborations with Tricky Stewart, The-Dream, and Midi Mafia on the EP release, Bieber adds to his production and songwriting team with Grammy-winning songwriter and producer Bryan-Michael Cox and The Stereotypes (whose previous artists include Mary J Blige and Ne-Yo).

My World 2.0 debuted at No. 1 on the US *Billboard* 200, selling over 280,000 copies in its first week.

The album's lead single *Baby*, featuring Ludacris, is the most watched video in *YouTube*'s history with a whopping 785 million views. The single, which was released on January 18, 2010, fuses a variety of genres from the expected R&B and pop styles to Fifties doo-wop which is evident in the opening vocal melody.

My World 2.0 echoes influences of various genres including Motown, dance, and disco.

■ **ABOVE:** Ryan Seacrest presents Justin with the Artist of the Year award at the 38th annual American Music Awards, November 2010.

19

My Worlds: The Collection

Following the success of *My World* and *My World 2.0* JB's compilation album, aptly named *My Worlds: The Collection*, was released on November 19, 2010. Consisting of two discs, fans were able to get their hands on a copy of the new slightly altered version of *My Worlds Acoustic* as well as the compilation album itself made up of the two previous releases. *Pray*, *Never Say Never*, and remixes of *Somebody To Love* were also included.

Pray was well received by critics and fans alike, and was the album's first and only single to be released. The message that the song holds is of pain and suffering in the world. The music video enhances this message with clips of natural disaster, sick children, and poverty. While the song itself is primarily of a contemporary Christian genre, pop and R&B undertones are evident. While in an interview with *American Idol* and US radio host Ryan Seacrest, Justin said that the song was written with Michael Jackson's *Man In The Mirror* in mind.

Track Listing:
Disc 1:
One Time (acoustic version)
Baby (acoustic version)
One Less Lonely Girl (acoustic version)
Down To Earth (acoustic version)
U Smile (acoustic version)
Stuck In The Moment (acoustic version)
Favorite Girl (live)
That Should Be Me (acoustic version)
Never Say Never (acoustic version) (ft. Jaden Smith)
Pray
Somebody To Love (ft. Usher)
Never Say Never (ft. Jaden Smith)
Somebody To Love (j-Stax remix)

Disc 2: *My Worlds*
One Time
Favorite Girl
Down To Earth
Bigger
One Less Lonely Girl
First Dance
Love Me
Common Denominator
Baby (ft. Ludacris)
Somebody To Love
Stuck In The Moment
U Smile
Runaway Love
Never Let You Go
Overboard (ft. Jessica Jarrell)
Eenie Meenie (with Sean Kingston)
Up
That Should Be Me

■ **OPPOSITE ABOVE:** Usher congratulates Justin for winning the award for Artist of the Year at the 38th annual American Music Awards.

■ **OPPOSITE BELOW:** Justin with Jaden Smith.

■ **BELOW:** Backstage in the press room at the MTV Video Music Awards in 2010.

My Worlds Acoustic

My Worlds Acoustic was the first remix album to be released by Justin Bieber. Released on November 26, 2010 the album was initially only available at Walmart stores and Sam's Club in the US. It features nine acoustic versions of songs previously heard on *My World* and *My World 2.0*. After the initial exclusive release via Walmart, the album became available on iTunes in February 2011.

In an interview with MTV Justin said: *"I really think that I did an acoustic album because there's a lot of haters out there that say, 'Justin Bieber can't sing. His voice is all Auto-Tuned.' And there's a lot with production, it kind of drowns out your voice, and it takes away from the singer, over the synths and everything.*

"I think kind of stripping it down," he added, *"and having it kind of really mellow and being able to hear my voice is why I wanted to do it."*

As part of the album promotion, as well as promoting his 3D movie, JB shot an alternative music video for the acoustic rendition of the song *Never Say Never*. The video premiered during Game 3 of the 2010 World Series and Justin also performed the song for the first time at the 2010 American Music Awards.

Track Listing:

One Time
Baby
One Less Lonely Girl
Down To Earth
U Smile
Stuck In The Moment
Favorite Girl (live)
That Should Be Me
Never Say Never (ft. Jaden Smith)
Pray

Never Say Never: The Remixes

Never Say Never: The Remixes was released on February 14, 2011 and was the second remix album to be released by the star. Accompanying the release of his movie *Justin Bieber: Never Say Never*, the album includes remixes of songs from his first album. Featuring artists such as Miley Cyrus, Kanye West, and Chris Brown, the album reached No. 1 on the US *Billboard* 200 chart and was certified Platinum by the RIAA.

The album's opening track *Never Say Never* is a collaboration between Justin and Jaden Smith and was the theme song for *The Karate Kid* (2010). It later became the album's lead single, which was released on January 25, 2011.

Track Listing:

Never Say Never (ft. Jaden Smith)

That Should Be Me (remix) (ft. Rascal Flatts)
Somebody To Love (remix) (ft. Usher)
Up (remix) (ft. Chris Brown)
Overboard (live) (ft. Miley Cyrus)
Runaway Love (Kanye West remix) (ft. Kanye West and Raekwon)
Born To Be Somebody

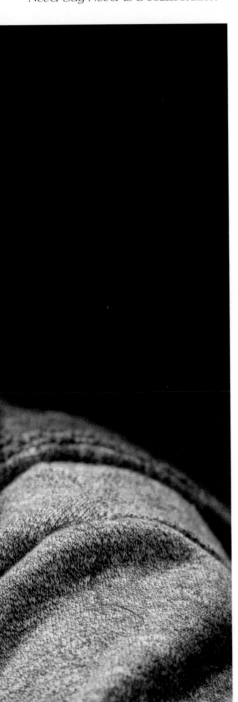

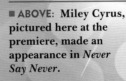

■ **ABOVE: Miley Cyrus, pictured here at the premiere, made an appearance in *Never Say Never*.**

■ **OPPOSITE: Justin smiles during a news conference for *Justin Bieber: Never Say Never* in Toronto.**

23

Under The Mistletoe

Released: November 1, 2010
No. 1 in Canada and the
United States
Canada: Certified Triple Platinum
United States: Certified Platinum
Australia: Certified Gold

On November 1, 2010, Justin Bieber released his second studio album. The Christmas album, titled *Under The Mistletoe*, featured many artist collaborations including Taylor Swift, Sean Kingston, and Mariah Carey. The eagerly awaited album, which had been announced earlier in the year, debuted straight in at No. 1 on the US *Billboard* 200 selling more than 200,000 copies in its first week. Ready to pounce on another record title, JB's album became the first Christmas album by a male artist to debut in at No. 1. If that's not enough, JB is also the first solo artist in *Billboard* history to have three No. 1 albums before his 18th birthday.

The festive album was well received worldwide, debuting within the top 10 in Spain, The Netherlands, Norway, and Australia.

Written and produced by The Messengers, the first single *Mistletoe* was released on October 17, 2010 in order to promote the forthcoming album.

Track Listing:

*Only Thing I Ever Get
For Christmas
Mistletoe
The Christmas Song (Chestnuts
Roasting On An Open Fire)*
(ft. Usher)
*Santa Claus Is Coming To Town
Fa La La* (ft. Boyz II Men)
*All I Want For Christmas Is
You (SuperFestive!)* (duet with
Mariah Carey)

Drummer Boy (ft. Busta Rhymes)
*Christmas Eve
All I Want Is You
Home This Christmas*
(ft. The Band Perry)
Silent Night

In addition to the standard album release, deluxe editions of the album were available which featured acoustic and cappella versions of his tracks. The Indonesian release also contained a DVD with exclusive content of music videos and studio footage.

■ BELOW: Sean Kingston
and Justin.

25

■ ABOVE: Justin pictured
with Taylor Swift.

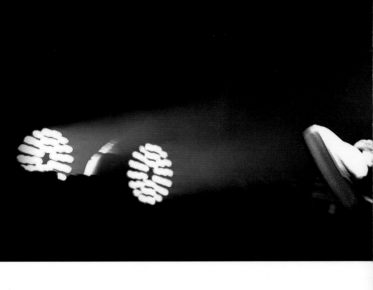

JustinBieber

Released: June 15, 2012
Top 10 in United States, Canada, Australia, Austria, France, Ireland, United Kingdom, New Zealand
Canada: Certified Double Platinum
Australia: Certified Double Platinum
United States: Certified Platinum
New Zealand: Certified Gold

Believe is the third studio album recorded by Justin Bieber and was released on June 15, 2012. The album debuted at No. 1 on the US *Billboard* 200, selling 347,000 copies in its first week – the biggest debut sales week for an album sold in 2012.

Selling 57,000 copies in its first week in Canada led to *Believe* topping the album chart before dropping to No. 2 in the second week. In the United Kingdom, *Believe* debuted at No. 1 making Bieber the second youngest solo artist to reach the coveted top spot.

As Bieber has grown, so too has his music. The album marks a significant evolution from the previously heard teen-style pop/R&B into an altogether more mature sound. By collaborating with a wide variety of legendary producers including Max Martin, who, with a diverse history of music production and songwriting skills, has worked with the likes of Britney Spears, *NSYNC, Katy Perry, Taylor Swift, and Backstreet Boys, the album has a distinct dance/pop feel as well as holding onto the R&B roots.

Ensuring the album would be a hit, Bieber also enlisted producers Darkchild, Hit-Boy, and Diplo. Hit-Boy is known for his extensive work with artists such as Jay-Z, Rihanna, Snoop Dogg, and Chris Brown, while Darkchild had previously worked with Bieber's idol Michael Jackson.

When asked about the album *Believe* in an interview with *V Magazine*, Justin said: *"I'm not going to try to conform to what people want me to be or go out there and start partying, have people see me with alcohol. I want to do it at my own pace. I don't want to start singing about things like sex, drugs, and swearing. I'm into love, and maybe I'll get more into making love when I'm older. But I want to be someone who is respected by everybody."*

The album's lead single *Boyfriend* was released on March 26, 2012 and has been compared to early Justin Timberlake tracks and echoes a similar sound to *NSYNC's track *Girlfriend*. The track was a commercial success, selling over 550,000 copies in its first week. Prior to the single's release, Bieber posted two versions of the cover art on his website and encouraged fans to vote for their favorite. The most voted for artwork was then published as the official cover for the single.

On May 11, 2012 he released the song *Turn To You (Mother's Day Dedication)* with the proceeds of the song going to help single mothers. The track however, did not make it onto the album *Believe*.

The second single *As Long As You Love Me*, released on July 10, 2012, is an emotional song with a dub-step edge. Produced by Darkchild and featuring Big Sean, *As Long As You Love Me* was previously released as a promotional single in June as a lead up to the album release.

■ ABOVE: The 2012 MuchMusic Video Awards
in Toronto.

29

Released on November 12, 2012, *Beauty And A Beat* is the only song on the album that was not co-written by Justin Bieber. Featuring the guest vocals of Nicki Minaj, the up-tempo electro-dance track mentions Selena Gomez in the female rap section. Promotion for the music video was cleverly and deviously planned.

Following a performance at the Tacoma Dome on October 9, 2012, Justin Bieber took to Facebook and Twitter to announce that both he and his manager, Scooter Braun, had personal property stolen. The singer reported that his laptop and camera had been burgled while he was in concert and that he was later targeted on Twitter by the alleged laptop thief who threatened to leak private footage on *YouTube*. Fans witnessed the "thief" state on Twitter that at noon on October 12, 2012 they would leak a major and potentially career-threatening video supposedly found on the laptop.

Thousands of avid fans followed the link that was later put out to find the music video to *Beauty And A Beat*. The clever "hoax" marketing ploy was a tremendous success. The *YouTube* video reached a massive seven million views in less than 24 hours. Many fans know that Justin Bieber is a fan of a good prank, and he certainly pulled that one off.

Track Listing:

All Around The World (ft. Ludacris)
Boyfriend
As Long As You Love Me (ft. Big Sean)
Take You
Right Here (ft. Drake)
Catching Feelings
Fall
Die In Your Arms
Thought Of You
Beauty And A Beat (ft. Nicki Minaj)
One Love
Be Alright
Believe
Out Of Town Girl
She Don't Like The Lights
Maria

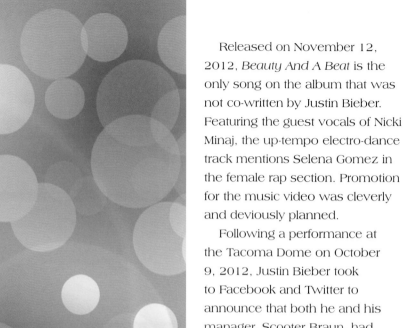

■ **OPPOSITE ABOVE: Justin and Selena Gomez in the audience at the 2011 MTV Video Music Awards.**

■ **OPPOSITE BELOW: Justin with rapper Ludacris.**

Tours

The Urban Behavior Tour (2009)

Being an international sensation, Justin is no stranger to global travel for both performance and promotion. During his first release, he was able to get his first taste of touring with a short stint in his home country. The five-date tour, sponsored by Urban Behavior, included dates in Vancouver, Montreal, London, Edmonton, and Toronto.

Although his first tour was very short and didn't push him beyond his home country, Bieber was busy actively promoting his debut single and album internationally. During the summer and fall of 2009, he visited a variety of TV and radio stations including Radio Disney and American Top 40.

Television appearances included presenting the 2009 MTV Video Music Awards and appearing as a special guest on YTV's MuchMusic. Talk shows also became very familiar for the rising star as he appeared and performed on popular shows such as the *Ellen DeGeneres Show*, *It's On with Alexa Chung*, *Lopez Tonight*, and *Good Morning America*. On December 10, 2009 he appeared on BET's *106 & Park* alongside international R&B pop star Rihanna.

His performance at *The Today Show Toyota Concert Series* was eagerly awaited by his adoring fans, many of whom camped out for 32 hours prior to the show and were thrilled when Justin went out to surprise them. JB's international appearances included a performance on the German TV show *The Dome* and the UK's BBC show *Blue Peter*. He had previously also appeared

■ **ABOVE & BELOW: Justin performs on NBC's *Today* show.**

■ **ABOVE: Justin at Nickelodeon's 23rd Annual Kids' Choice Awards.**

on *The X Factor* in the UK, where he famously asked fellow singer and then judge Cheryl Cole to phone him.

Bieber also had the privilege of performing Stevie Wonder's *Someday At Christmas* for President Barack Obama and First Lady Michelle Obama at the White House for a televised music special *Christmas in Washington*, which was aired on December 20, 2009.

My World Tour (2010)

As he did with *My World*, Justin Bieber went on a radio promotion spree in addition to other international appearances to promote his album *My World*

2.0. On March 5, 2010 Justin performed at The Dome 53 in Berlin and later returned to Germany as part of his global tour. He performed a concert at Houston Rodeo alongside Selena Gomez on March 21, which was closely followed by appearances on ABC's *Nightline* and *CBS News*. Then, on March 27, he performed at the 2010 Kids' Choice Awards.

It was a busy month for Justin

■ ABOVE: Justin performing live on CBS's *The Early Show*.

Bieber when he announced in March 2010 that his first world tour would commence on June 23. With 130 shows planned and a whole host of support acts and special guests, Bieber was intent on making his first world tour one to remember.

Supporting acts included Sean Kingston, The Stunners, and The Wanted. J-Beebs also thrilled the crowds with his impressive guest star appearances from Usher, Boyz II Men, Ludacris, and Akon to name but a few.

The tour made over $53 million worldwide, not bad for a first global tour!

The tour was a raging success with critics giving positive reviews of Bieber's performances. Justin used his gigs as an opportunity to promote important messages such as anti-bullying and "don't text and drive." Fans were thrilled and impressed as JB wowed them with break dancing, piano playing, drum soloing, and rapping. He certainly proved his many talents.

Believe Tour (2012-13)

In May 2012, it was announced that Justin Bieber would be kicking off his second world tour for his album *Believe* on September 29. With 88 shows to perform between September 2012 and May 2013, the Believe tour was not to prove as hectic as his previous world tour.

Carly Rae Jepsen, Usher, and Jaden Smith were some of the celebrities that made guest appearances. The average revenue for each show was a massive $1,000,000 with 100% of tickets for each show sold out.

On the opening night of the tour, Justin paid tribute to six-year-old Avalanna Routh, the cancer patient he had made a special bond with earlier in the year. The little girl had suffered from an Atypical Teratoid Rhabdoid Tumor (ATRT), a rare incurable brain cancer that sadly took her life only days before the *Believe* tour commenced.

Unlike previous shows, where Justin invited a girl from the crowd for his performance of *One Less Lonely Girl* and presented her with flowers, he dedicated the song to Avalanna while a photomontage was shown on screen. He rounded the performance off by placing the bouquet of flowers on an empty seat.

Fans may also remember the opening show at Glendale, Arizona for JB's onstage sickness. The singer vomited on stage during his performance of *Out Of Town Girl*. Despite this, Justin soldiered on for the rest of the show and thanked his fans for their support. He later tweeted: *"Milk was a bad choice."*

On October 9, 2012 during the Tacoma Dome performance in Washington, J-Biebs and his manager were left furious after a camera and laptop containing personal footage were stolen. To add further worry, the unidentified thief then tweeted Justin Bieber threatening to leak footage. The media jumped on the story and shocked Beliebers nervously waited to see what the "thief" would do...

Of course, we all now know that the theft was all part of the clever marketing ploy to promote the upcoming launch of *Beauty And A Beat*, featuring Nicki Minaj, as the "thief" leaked out a never-before-seen music video for the song.

In true charitable Justin Bieber style, the singer donated a portion of the profits from the *Believe* tour to help build schools in third-world countries.

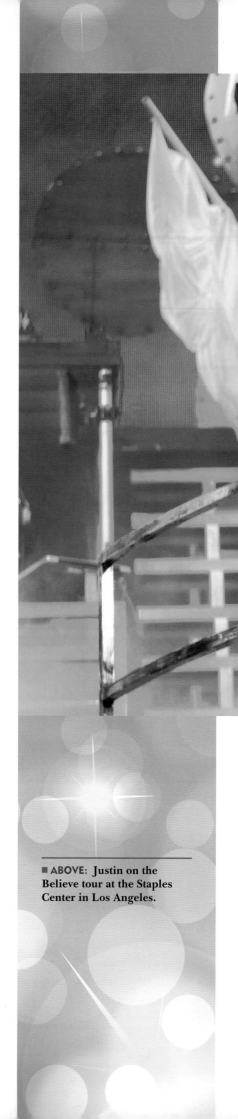

■ **ABOVE: Justin on the Believe tour at the Staples Center in Los Angeles.**

Justin Bieber: Never Say Never

Release date: February 11, 2011
Budget: Estimated $13,000,000
Opening Weekend: $29,514,054
(United States)
Gross: $73,000,942
(United States)

In August 2010, news escaped that Justin Bieber was working on a feature-length biopic, which would give fans a true insight into the 10 days leading up to his sold-out show at Madison Square Garden in the US.

Footage included rehearsals, concerts from the My World tour, life behind the scenes, and family life as well as clips of home movies, photos, and interviews showing the young singer and how he had developed into an astounding international pop star. The cast was made up of Justin's entourage, as well as other notable celebrities including Miley Cyrus, Jaden Smith, Sean Kingston, Ludacris, and Snoop Dogg.

Close family and friends are also interviewed including Justin's mother and grandparents. The movie was designed to give fans (and non-fans alike) the opportunity to see what life is like while on tour for the singer. It gives the viewer another perspective of Bieber who, while making a visit to his hometown, is scolded for damaging his voice when he met up with old friends.

The movie was due to be directed by Academy Award-winning director Davis Guggenheim but, with the upcoming promotion for *Waiting for Superman*, Guggenheim dropped out of the directing position for the movie. Jon Chu, best known for directing *Step Up 3D*, was then recruited to direct the movie. Chu is said to have leapt at the opportunity to tell the story in a compelling and genuine way, saying that Bieber had a "true underdog story."

Chu said, when speaking about the plot idea for the movie, *"We had this sort of hyperlink idea through the movie, which is what makes it really an interesting movie. It's not like the other concert movies where you are onstage and then go backstage and then onstage and go backstage. It's not just the concert... this is a musical movie, when words aren't enough in telling the stories of his life, [we use music]."*

On August 24, 2010 Justin took to Twitter to announce to fans that they could enter a competition to be part of the movie. The contest, which was only open for 24 hours, involved fans sending in home movies of themselves singing *That Should Be Me* or by sending in photos to represent *U Smile*.

J-Biebs also announced

another contest in December 2010; loyal fans that purchased the special screening package would be automatically entered into a competition, which would see five lucky contestants fly out to join the singer at the premiere. The special screening package included a souvenir lanyard, glowstick, bracelet, and 3D glasses.

Filming for the movie took place on August 31, 2010 at the Madison Square Garden concert where JB wore his purple and white tour attire. In addition to performing the set list, Sean Kingston, Jaden Smith, Boyz II Men, Usher, and Miley Cyrus all appeared and performed songs with Justin.

As part of the promotion for the upcoming movie, for which the title was not currently known, Jon Chu tweeted Bieber's fans about an internet scavenger hunt to seek out the unknown title of the movie. Celebrities including Ryan Seacrest and Ellen DeGeneres revealed clues to help fans solve the puzzle. The final clue was tweeted by *USA Today* and the title of the movie, *Justin Bieber: Never Say Never* was disclosed.

On the first day of the trailer's release, Justin surprised fans by giving them the first look at his Los Angeles concert on October 26.

Released in time for Valentine's Day, *Justin Bieber: Never Say Never* topped the Friday box office with an estimated $12.4 million on its opening day.

The movie exceeded industry expectations, nearly matching the $31 million grossing movie *Hannah Montana & Miley Cyrus*, the 2008 3D concert movie, which holds the record for top debut for a music documentary. *Never Say Never* grossed higher in its first weekend than the 2009 concert movie *Michael Jackson's This Is It*. The movie also made more than double that made by *Jonas Brothers: The 3D Concert Experience*. With worldwide sales reaching over $98 million, in the United States it is the highest grossing music concert movie of all time.

On February 25, 2011 a limited edition alternative version of the movie was re-released in 3D movie theaters in Canada and the United States. *Never Say Never – Director's Fan Cut* had 40 minutes of new unseen footage. The movie was released on DVD and Blu-ray on May 13, 2011 in the US.

To promote the release of the movie a pseudo-holiday was created called *NSN Weekend* as part of an online viral marketing campaign. As a countdown to *NSN Weekend* a micro-site featuring a ticking clock was created prompting fans to sign up via Facebook and RSVP to a global viewing event. Each day all the RSVP fans were able to get their hands on "party favors" such as life-size posters of JB, a Bieber-Berry cupcake recipe, and never-before-seen concert clips. The campaign resulted in 10,000 downloads of Justin Bieber swag, 242 million overall social impressions, and over 40,000 clicks to buy the movie.

■ **ABOVE LEFT: Justin with his sister Jazmyn, father Jeremy, and mother Pattie prior to the screening of his movie in Toronto.**

■ **LEFT: Portia de Rossi, Justin, and Ellen DeGeneres at the 2012 Teen Choice Awards.**

39

Awards

With Justin Bieber being an international superstar selling more than 15 million albums, it's unsurprising that the singer has earned himself 74 awards in the short time that he has been a global sensation.

In 2010 he won four awards at the American Music Awards including Artist of the Year, Favorite Pop/Rock Male Artist, T-Mobile Breakthrough Artist, and *My World* won Favorite Pop/Rock Album.

He also scooped three awards at the J-14 Teen Icon Awards; being an avid user of social networking, it was fitting that JB won the Iconic Tweeter award. He also won Iconic Male Star and his hit song *Baby* won the Iconic Song award. *Baby* also won the MTV Video Music award for Best New Artist.

Justin Bieber grabbed another handful of MTV awards in 2010 including International Artist at the MTV Video Music Brazil and Best Male and Best Push Act at the MTV Europe Music Awards. The MuchMusic Video Awards, presented by Canadian music channel MuchMusic, awarded J-Biebs with UR FAVE New Artist, and *Baby* scooped both the UR FAVE Canadian Video and International Video of the Year by a Canadian.

Bieber also won Newcomer of the Year at the Young Hollywood Awards, and at the Teen Choice Awards bagged himself a further four awards including Choice Music: Male Artist, Choice Music: Breakout Artist Male, and Choice Summer Music Star: Male.

After a successful 2010, 2011 proved to be no different with the star scooping another coveted clutch of awards.

In February that year, Bieber won International Breakthrough

Act at the BRIT Awards in the UK. J-Biebs then took an impressive six awards from the *Billboard* Music Awards in May 2011 including Top New Artist, Top Social Artist, Top Streaming Artist, and Top Digital Media Artist proving once again that he truly is a star of the digital age. His album *My World 2.0* scooped Top Pop Album and *Baby* was awarded Top Streaming Song (Video).

Justin Bieber was also nominated for Best New Artist and Best Pop Vocal Album (*My World 2.0*) at the prestigious Grammy Awards annually held by the National Academy of Recording Arts and Sciences. Unfortunately Bieber didn't win as Bon Iver and Adele won those awards respectively.

However, Justin was more successful at the Juno Awards, the Canadian music ceremony, presented by the Canadian

Academy of Recorded Arts and Sciences, when he won two of the four awards he had been nominated for. *My World 2.0* won Pop Album of the Year and JB was also awarded with the Fan Choice award.

Kicking off 2012, Justin Bieber won the NRJ Award of Honor. The NRJ Music Awards was created in 2000 by radio station NRJ in partnership with the television network TF1. The annual awards ceremony takes place each year in mid-January in Cannes, France at the opening of MIDEM, the world's largest music industry trade fair. Nominated for five awards, JB proudly took the Top Social Artist award at the *Billboard Music Awards* in May. For the second year in a row he also won the Fan Choice award at the Juno Awards. Then, for the third year in a row, Bieber scooped the Choice Music: Male Artist at the Teen Choice Awards. He also won Choice Red Carpet Fashion Icon Male, Choice Summer Music Star Male, and his *NSYNC-inspired track *Boyfriend* won Choice Music Single by a Male Artist.

■ **ABOVE:** Justin poses with some Mounties as he arrives at the 2010 Juno Awards in St. John's, Newfoundland, Canada.

■ **ABOVE:** Usher and Justin at the 53rd annual Grammy Awards, 2011.

■ **LEFT:** Receiving the award for International Breakthrough Act at the BRIT Awards 2011.

■ **OPPOSITE:** Justin arrives at the Cannes Festival Palace, to take part in the NRJ Music Awards ceremony.

Born To Be Somebody

■ ABOVE: Justin switches on the Christmas lights at Westfield London, with young teens from the Teenage Cancer Trust.

Justin**Bieber**

Charity Drive

With the young international superstar earning more in one sponsorship deal than most people would earn in a lifetime, you'd expect to see some extravagant spending, but what may come as a surprise is the amount of charities that Justin supports and promotes.

Far from being just another rich teen pop star, J-Beebs proves to the world that he is also a young man trying to improve and enrich the lives of others. In fact, he supports over 20 charities, often donating his own money and spending time and effort with fundraising campaigns and raising awareness. Just a handful of the charities he actively supports include the Teenage Cancer Trust, Red Cross, Children's Miracle Network Hospitals, and Food Bank for New York City. The list goes on and includes many international and cultural causes.

His Believe Charity Drive encourages fans to start their own fundraiser and has managed to raise more than $1 million already. While on the My World tour, Justin made time to visit 86 Make a Wish children: one child for every concert in North America.

In the lead up to the release of his Christmas album, *Under*

■ RIGHT: Justin attends a lighting ceremony at the Empire State Building in honor of the Marine Toys for Tots Foundation.

The Mistletoe, Justin announced that a portion of the profits would be donated to seven different charities.

So which charities did he support with his Christmas album?

Make-A-Wish Foundation

The Make-A-Wish Foundation makes dreams come true for children with life-threatening conditions.

Pencils Of Promise

The Pencils Of Promise mission is to create schools, programs, and global communities around the common goal of education for all. They believe every child should have access to quality education.

Musicians On Call

Musicians On Call brings live and recorded music to the bedsides of patients in healthcare facilities. By transforming sterile hospital rooms into a vibrant stage, they bring joy and hope to patients.

City of Hope

Determined to lead the fight against cancer, diabetes, HIV/AIDS, and other life-threatening diseases, City of Hope aims to turn promising ideas into treatments.

Boys & Girls Club of America

The Boys & Girls Club of America aims to keep kids off the streets by offering safe and nurturing outlets, complete with mentors and after-school activities.

Project Medishare

Project Medishare is dedicated to providing comprehensive health and development services in Haiti. They operate a critical care and trauma hospital, intensive care units for sick babies and children, cholera treatment, and rural health clinics.

GRAMMY Foundation

The GRAMMY Foundation partners high school students with music professionals to get real-world industry experience and advice for those that want to pursue a career in the music industry.

Winter 2011 was a generous time for JB, who in true festive spirit also went on to donate $500,000 to the *Children's Wish Foundation.* He presented the check to the charity at the end of the Christmas TV special *Home for the Holidays,* which was held in Toronto. While in the area, Justin also took the time to stop off at a food bank that, as a young boy, had been familiar to him. He donated $10,000 to the *Stratford House of Blessing,* the food bank he and his mom would visit in hard times when a holiday meal was too expensive for the family.

Generosity is something that comes naturally to JB, when earlier in the year while on the *Ellen DeGeneres Show* he said he'd make a $100,000 donation to the Whitney Elementary School in Las Vegas after the school's story had been featured earlier in the year on the show. The Whitney School, located in Nevada, has one of the highest populations of homeless children in the area and helps underprivileged children and their families by helping with bills, and offering clothing and food.

■ **RIGHT:** Justin performs during the SOS Saving Ourselves – Help for Haiti – benefit.

49

In addition to the $100,000 check that was made (from his own account) JB went on to thrill hundreds of the school's students by performing a private concert during his charitable visit. If that wasn't generous enough, the teen then went on to treat the students to $100,000 worth of Christmas gifts.

Feeling charitable and festive, and to round it all off, Justin also adopted a puppy with his girlfriend Selena Gomez. With all this in mind, it's not surprising to hear that Justin Bieber was HuffPost Impact's most charitable celeb of 2011.

Fans of J-Beeb will also be familiar with his Charity: Water Campaign. Following the success of the fundraising idea for his 17th birthday, which raised $47,148, JB again announced that his 18th birthday wish was to raise money for the charity, which aims to provide clean, safe water for villages in developing nations.

But Justin's charitable giving goes way beyond handing out checks and promoting worthy charities. This is a young man who has taken the time to visit sick children's hospitals and meet cancer patients. The most touching story is that of the aforementioned Avalanna Routh, the six-year-old girl who was battling with an aggressive and rare form of cancer.

Avalanna had been desperate to meet her favorite pop star and upon hearing of the little girl's wish via Facebook, Bieber flew Avalanna and her family out to New York on Valentine's Day for a surprise encounter. The pair spent the day playing board games and eating cupcakes. Spending the day with her pop idol was a dream come true for the little girl. Afterward, Bieber wrote on

Twitter: "*That was one of the best things I have ever done. She was AWESOME! Feeling really inspired now! #MrsBieber really inspired me.*"

The ATRT cancer that Avalanna was suffering from is so rare that less than 30 new cases of the cancer are diagnosed in the US each year and, sadly, there is no known cure.

On September 26, 2012 Justin found out from Avalanna's mom that the little girl had lost her battle against this aggressive and incurable cancer and had passed away. Upon hearing the tragic news, Justin shared his sorrow with his fans on Twitter writing: "*Just got the worst news*

ever. One of the greatest spirits I have ever known is gone. Please pray for her family and for her. RIP Avalanna. I love you." He then posted a picture of the two of them together from his visit, calling Avalanna his angel.

At the Arizona concert on September 29, 2012 Justin dedicated the song *One Less Lonely Girl* to Avalanna, who had become known as Mrs Bieber, and later tweeted: "*Goodnight Avalanna. Tonight was for u. I love u.*"

■ **ABOVE: Justin waves to fans in front of Whitney Elementary School.**

■ ABOVE: Justin kisses his girlfriend, Selena Gomez, during an NBA basketball game as the San Antonio Spurs play the Los Angeles Lakers, April, 2012.

■ LEFT: Justin autographs a guitar on a surprise visit to high school summer band camp students at Seminole High School in Sanford, August, 2010. Justin's sponsors, Best Buy Company Inc. and the Grammy Foundation, donated $5,000 to the high school music program.

Bieber Fever

Soon after the arrival of Justin Bieber in the public eye, lots of Bieber-related words swept the nation. Fans, or "Beliebers" would scream in a frenzy of excitement. This act of over-excitement, swooning, and excessive screaming soon became publically known and used in media headlines as Bieber Fever. However, as amusing and light-hearted as the media titles sounded, Bieber Fever that gripped teens and pre-teens, got out of control on several occasions.

As part of the *My World* EP promotion, JB was scheduled to perform at Roosevelt Field Mall in Long Island. Over 3,000 excited fans had camped out in order to catch the singer's performance and CD signing, but chaos soon reigned as the screaming fans stampeded out of control. Several

people were hurt and one fan ended up in the hospital as a result of the sudden surge in the crowd.

The police arrested an Island Records senior vice-president James A Roppo for hindering their crowd control efforts. Bieber took to Twitter to tell his fans of the cancelled performance tweeting: *"The event at Roosevelt Mall is cancelled. Please go home. The police have already arrested one person from my camp. I don't want anyone hurt."*

Biebermania vs Beatlemania

Biebermania is said to have hit the UK while J-Biebs was in Liverpool, a city known for being the hometown of the legendary band, The Beatles.

The singer was due to perform at the Liverpool Echo Arena in March 2011 and fans had heard that he was in the city prior to his concert.

The scenes of over-excited fans were reminiscent of the frenzy that met The Beatles wherever they went in the early 1960s. The police were called in to control a large crowd of girls who had gathered outside the Hard Days Night hotel where the singer was staying. So, police were forced to close a central city street for over five hours until the

53

crowd dispersed.

The hysteria that comes with Bieber Fever doesn't end there; at an appearance in Australia, 10 teenage fans fainted and eight girls were hospitalized. Beliebers have also chased the singer through airports, and thousands of fans became unruly when Bieber visited Oslo, Norway.

The actions of Beliebers have escalated in some situations where they strongly defend the singer. When Esperanza Spalding won a Grammy over JB, fans attacked her on Facebook and Twitter. Bieber fans also vandalized Spalding's page on Wikipedia. Their behavior further intensified when they started to threaten Grammy judges.

Anti-Beliebers

As with any global superstar, Justin Bieber has had more than his fair share of "haters" and has had to deal with a variety of situations and issues. Along with the usual pessimists and slander, Justin has had lawsuits and even a paternity suit to face.

A woman filed a $9.2 million lawsuit against JB after she claimed that she suffered permanent hearing loss following a concert in July 2010. Stacey Wilson Betts insisted that the frenzy of screams encouraged by the singer resulted in her getting severe tinnitus and hyperacusis. Also named in the lawsuit was his label, Island Def Jam, and Vulcan Sports and Entertainment, where the concert was held in Portland.

In 2011, Mariah Yeater claimed that the singer was the father of her baby boy, after she and JB met and had a backstage encounter. Yeater's lawyers withdrew the lawsuit, although

■ABOVE: **Mariah Yeater holds baby Tristyn during an interview on** *The Insider*. **She claimed Justin fathered her child and went on television to defend her accusations.**

access more content if they choose to subscribe to the yearly option. The site also has its very own Twitter page that has more than 308,000 followers.

Along with tour information, news, and the fan site community, subscribers can enter contests and grab themselves early bird tickets to upcoming shows and offers. Fans are also offered the opportunity to bag themselves JB branded swag when they become a member and can add continually to their Bieber branded merchandise for each year they subscribe.

they said that the case was not dismissed and that they would settle the matter out of court. The paternity case was described as "completely out of control" when Yeater had been flooded with abusive threats and was harassed by Beliebers while trying to walk through the park with her baby. Bieber took the paternity test to prove he was not the child's father.

Fan Sites

Justin Bieber has some of the most dedicated fans following his every triumph and success. Some of the major Beliebers have committed themselves to many hours of hard work to create some of the most resourceful online fan sites dedicated to the singer, for all Beliebers to enjoy.

These sites contain everything Bieber-related including snippets of gossip, news, photos, music and video clips, tour information, lyrics, and online polls. Many sites also have challenging quizzes and games to test the knowledge of JB's fans. Ultimately these sites have become a forum for fellow Beliebers to chat about their pop idol.

In addition to the fan-created sites, there is of course the official Bieber-packed fan site "Bieber Fever." The paid membership-driven site provides subscribers with different membership packages allowing the user to

55

Spending Power

Clothes and holidays

With a net worth of around $112 million, and annual earnings of around $53 million, it's not surprising to see that the global celebrity has enjoyed his hard-earned cash with a bit of spending, and who can blame

him? J-Biebs has sold over 15 million albums worldwide and earns an average of $300,000 per concert.

For Justin Bieber it's not all just about the music; as with other major celebrities, there's another powerful potential when fame strikes. He was paid a staggering $1 million to wear a space suit

alongside Ozzy Osbourne in the retail giant Best Buy commercial, which was transmitted at the US Super Bowl. His fresh-faced looks also led to him gaining the two-year deal endorsing the acne treatment ProActiv, bagging him a very tidy $3 million, and to top up his income he has put his name on a bed linen range, children's

jewelry, and headphones.

So let's take a sneaky peek at some of the things that J-Biebs has splashed the cash on since his rocketing rise to fame.

The romantic singer has been known to buy an entire florist's worth of flowers to dazzle girlfriend Selena Gomez. He has even chartered a helicopter to fly the pair over Toronto enabling Justin and Selena the opportunity to take in the sight from "a bird's eye view." The vacations don't end there though and with J-Biebs being a fan of Florida, he has been spotted in the area on several occasions, and has visited St Lucia for romantic retreats in the Caribbean with Selena, and the Bahamas where he has been seen enjoying the beaches and jeep safaris.

JB is also a fan of clothing brands such as Make Believe and can often be seen sporting the brand's clothes. Moving onto the star's "bling," the singer owns a Jacob and Co. diamond encrusted whistle worth a staggering $34,000 and was also reported to have spent $25,000 on a *Family Guy* "Stewie" pendant.

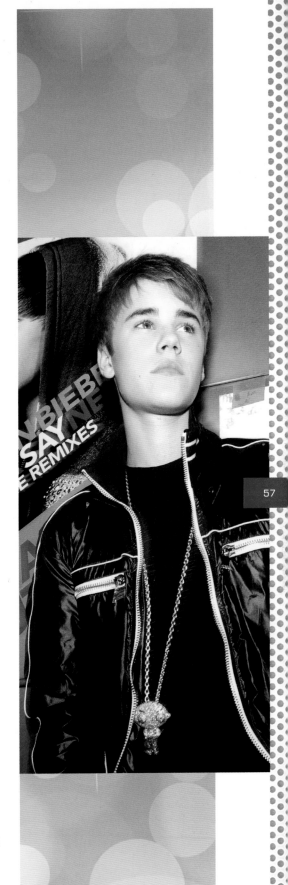

Cars

Where would any world-famous superstar be without his impressive collection of cars? Most 18 year olds are scraping funds together to buy their first motor, JB on the other hand has a collection of vehicles that would make most petrol heads feel green with envy...

Porsche 997 Turbo

Justin Bieber owns some of the most extravagant cars around and is often spotted cruising in

- ■ **ABOVE: Porsche 997 Turbo*.**
- ■ **LEFT: Cadillac CTS-V Coupe*.**
- ■ **BELOW: Lamborghini Gallardo*.**

*Not Justin's actual cars, just examples.

his Porsche 997 Turbo – a car that is cherished by many of the rich and famous. Powered by a 3.6-liter engine, the car can reach the 124mph mark in 12.8 seconds. Nice.

Lamborghini Gallardo

This mother of all supercars was a gift from pal P Diddy. The car, which is worth over $200,000, was promised to J-Biebs when he turned 16. Powered by a 5.0-liter V10 engine, not to mention its exquisite style, it's clear to see why the Lambo is one of Justin's favorite cars.

Smart Car aka Swag Car

The compact jet black Smart

Car is the only small-sized car in Bieber's car collection. Customized to suit JB's taste, the singer had the car's Smart Car logo swapped for the words "Swag Car."

Ducati 848 Evo

Despite not actually having a valid license for driving motorcycles, the singer splashed out on the white Ducati 848 Evo. Boasting a top speed of 170mph, the singer purchased the motorcycle on recommendation from his pal Usher.

Ferrari F430

Purchased when he was just 16, and worth over $250,000, the Ferrari F430 in metallic brown is one of the first supercars that Justin acquired.

Cadillac CTS-V Coupe

Customized to suit Justin's taste, the "Batmobile"-styled Cadillac certainly is an eye opener. A freshly re-sprayed black bodywork, crystal blue LED headlights, and luxury purple interior were all on the singer's wish list with this luxury new car.

Fisker Karma Hybrid Car

What does Justin Bieber get for his 18th birthday? A $100,000 car of course! The grand surprise from manager Scooter Braun and Usher was a Fisker Karma Hybrid Car. The car was presented to a very surprised Justin on the *Ellen DeGeneres Show*.

As well as being super stylish, this new smart car is eco friendly and comes equipped with a solar panel roof, and is powered by a 22-kilowatt-hour lithium battery. Of course, the singing sensation had to customize his new gift, which involved getting it wrapped in chrome and adding a strip of LEDs under the front grille.

After owning the car for less than six months, JB then gave it to Sean Kingston as a birthday present in September 2012.

Range Rover Evoque

The singer also owns a customized Range Rover Evoque, dishing out $160,000 for the vehicle. The interior of the car was designed by the Biebs and boasts an $80,000 sound system.

Houses

Calabasas

Justin's Calabasas home is a luxury six bedroom, seven bathroom dwelling, boasting a goliath-sized living room, superbly equipped kitchen, guest house, gorgeous swimming pool, and spa. Justin already plans to add a private theater and game room to his $6 million estate.

New York Apartment

Bought for him by his mother and grandmother for his 16th birthday, the lavishly decorated New York pad possesses three bedrooms and four bathrooms. Overlooking the city, the immense apartment features marble floors and a built-in wet bar with wine fridge.

Los Angeles Mansion

Situated in the Hollywood Hills, JB's mansion is built over three floors featuring five bedrooms, a gourmet kitchen, gym, movie theater, massage room, and infinity pool. The glass-walled house overlooks breathtaking views and set the star back a whopping $10.8 million.

■ **BELOW:** Sean Kingston, Selena Gomez, and Justin backstage at the Teen Choice Awards, 2011. Justin gave Sean the hybrid car.

Trivia, Quotes, and Quiz

World Record Breaking: The Facts

JB became the first solo artist in *Billboard* history to have at least four singles enter the top 40 of the Hot 100 before his debut album's release.

Bieber is the first solo artist to have three No. 1 albums before his 18th birthday. Justin is the youngest male solo artist to top the *Billboard* 200 chart for two or more weeks with his album *My World 2.0*, since Stevie Wonder's album *The Twelve Year Old Genius* in 1963.

In the second week, when *My World 2.0* sold even more copies, Bieber became the first artist since The Beatles to debut at No. 1 and sell more copies the following week.

The album's lead single, *Baby*, featuring Ludacris, is the most watched video in *YouTube* history with a whopping 785 million views.

Ready to pounce on another record title, JB's album became the first Christmas album by a male artist to debut in at No. 1.

J-Biebs' Inked Body

Justin got his first bit of ink on his left hip in March 2010 at the age of 16. Bieber's bird hip tattoo represents a seagull from the fable *Jonathan Livingston Seagull* and many of the male Bieber family members have the tattoo. The image represents "learning to fly."

Inked vertically down the singer's ribcage is Justin's second tattoo, "Yeshua" which means Jesus in Hebrew. It matches a tattoo that his father got in April 2011, during Justin's My World tour.

Being a devoted Christian, JB also has an image of Jesus on his left leg, depicting the crown of thorns and halo above Jesus' head.

Showing his religious side once again, there is a tattoo of praying hands inked in black and white on his left calf, just below the tattooed image of Jesus. During the *David Letterman Show* in June 2012, JB revealed another tattoo, this time inspired by his most recent album. On the inside of his left arm reads the word "Believe."

Shortly after revealing his Believe tattoo, the pop star got another; on his right arm is the inked Japanese symbol in the ancient Kanji style of writing, which translates to mean "music."

Last but not least, Justin had his crown tattoo inked on his chest just below his collarbone.

Justin Bieber's Acting Debut

The singer made his acting debut in season 11 of the popular TV crime series *CSI: Crime Scene Investigation.* Playing the part of troubled teen, Jason McCann, Bieber makes appearances in two episodes: *Shock Waves* and *Targets of Obsession.* Jason McCann, a serial bomber, is killed in the second episode.

An Expensive Lock of that Trademark Hair

How much would you pay for a lock of Bieb's hair? After Ellen DeGeneres said that all she wanted for her 53rd birthday was a bit of the singer's trademark fringe, Justin agreed to this on the

proviso that money raised from auctioning it off would be donated to charity. The lock of hair fetched an impressive $40,668 on eBay, all of which was donated to the animal charity Gentle Barn Foundation.

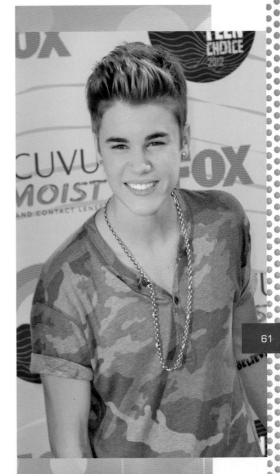

61

■ **BELOW: A scene from Justin's guest appearance on *CSI.***

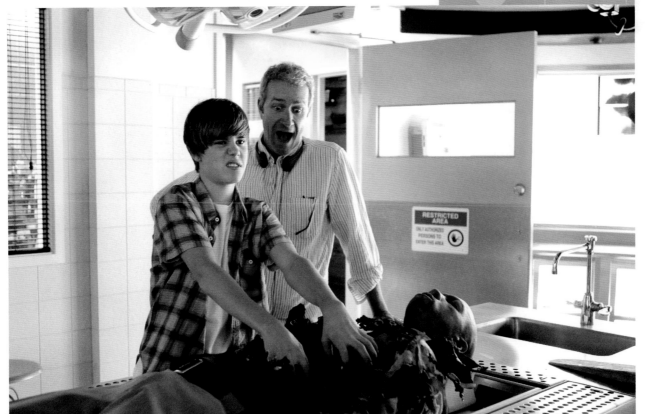

From the Mouth of Bieber: Quotes

"There's gonna be times in your life when people say you can't do something. And there's gonna be times in your life when people say that you can't live your dreams. This is what I tell them: never say never!"

"I'm a really claustrophobic person to begin with. I hate elevators, especially crammed elevators. I get really scared. So I think that it's very definitely scary when girls are all around me and I can't go anywhere. At the same time, I guess I got to get used to it, you know what I mean?"

"To all the haters out there I wish u the best. U can't bring me down. I wake up everyday grateful 4 the opportunity and grateful to the fans."

"It was like, Usher and Timberlake want to meet me? Are you kidding? There was no point in trying to tell anyone at school about this. It would be like telling them I was going to meet CHUCK NORRIS, and we all know that guy is untouchable. I mean, c'mon. It's CHUCK NORRIS. He doesn't need Twitter, he's already following you."

"I also try to read all of my fan mail. A lot of them send me candy, which I'm not allowed to eat 'cause my mom says it might be poisonous."

"Singers aren't supposed to have dairy before a show, but we all know I'm a rule breaker. Pizza is just so good!"

"There are lots of things I really like besides girls. Like pizza. And pranking. And CHUCK NORRIS."

"It was like I opened my eyes one day and noticed that the world was full of beautiful girls. And I've had a hard time thinking about anything else since then."

"I love that my fans are so devoted, because without them I wouldn't have this opportunity."

Are YOU JB's Biggest Belieber?

Take our Quiz and find out!

What is Justin's middle name?

What is Justin's star sign?

Who is JB's celebrity crush?

What is the name of Justin's favorite double-barreled clothing designer?

How much was the Family Guy "Stewie" pendant that JB bought?

What was the name of his first single?

What did he receive as an 18th birthday gift from manager Scooter Braun and mentor Usher?

True or False: Justin can play the drums?

Never Say Never is the soundtrack to what 2010 movie?

Justin guest starred as Jason McCann in what crime drama television series?

Answers
1. Drew
2. Pisces
3. Beyoncé
4. Make Believe
5. $25,000
6. One Time
7. Fisker Karma Hybrid Car
8. True
9. Karate Kid
10. CSI: Crime Scene Investigation